95

D0794580

OCT   2001

THE USBORNE BOOK OF
HAIR BRAIDING

Fiona Watt and Lisa Miles

Consultant: Jacki Wadeson • Hair stylist: Kathleen Bray
Designers: Maria Wheatley, Vicki Groombridge, Rachel Wells,
Kate Foyster and Kathy Ward
Illustrated by Chris Chaisty • Photographs by Ray Moller
Series editor: Cheryl Evans

Contents

With special thanks to: - Luke and Tom Ashby, Jahanara Chaudhri, Charlotte Crittenden,
Emily and Hannah Kirby-Jones, Marina Townsend, Francesca Tyler, Alexandra Varley-Winter,
Hannah Watts and Maddie York.

Simple braids

It only takes a little practice to become good at braiding. The simplest braid is a three-strand braid which you can wear as one braid or as two. **You will need:** brush, comb, covered bands.

You can add all kinds of accessories to hair once you have braided it.

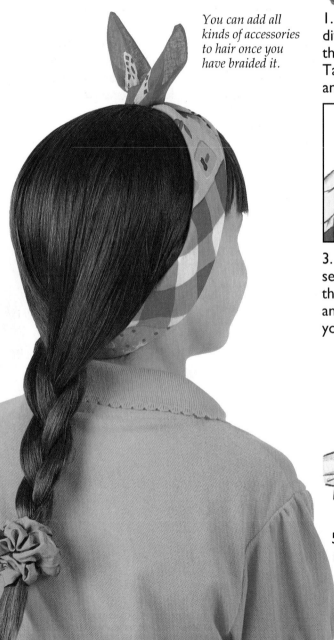

1. Use a comb to divide the hair into three equal sections. Take hold of the right and middle sections.

2. Cross your hands so the right section comes over the middle one and they swap places.

3. Hold the new right section between your thumb and first finger and the middle one in your other fingers.

4. Cross the left section over the middle one and take it in your right fingers. Swap the middle one to your left hand.

5. Cross the right section over the middle one again. Swap it to the fingers of your left hand.

6. Take the left section over the middle one, swapping it to the fingers of your right hand.

7. Continue braiding the hair by crossing the right section, then the left one over the middle section.

8. Near to the end of the sections, you may find it tricky to hold the hair in your fingers. Just grasp it tightly.

9. When you reach the end of the braid, hold the ends firmly between your first finger and thumb.

10. Slip a covered band over the end of the braid. Twist it around once to form a small loop at one side.

11. Put your fingers through the loop and pull the hair through, swapping the loop to your other hand.

12. If the band is still loose, twist and pull the hair through again. You may need to do this several times.

You can hide the covered band at the end of your braids with a ribbon or a scrunchie.

Braided bunches

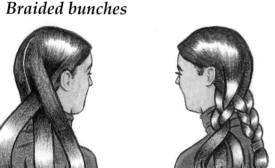

1. Use a comb to make a neat part down the back of the head. Push one side out of the way.

2. Divide one side into three sections. Braid the hair and secure it with a band. Repeat for the other side.

Hippie braids

You can make really bright, attractive braids by winding thread in different patterns around thin strands of hair. **You will need:** scissors, embroidery threads in contrasting shades.

Single braid

1. Cut two lengths of thread, about two and a half times as long as your hair. Tie them in a knot near to one end.

2. Use a comb to make a fine section of hair near to the front of your head. Hold the section firmly in one hand.

3. Loop the knotted end of the thread under the hair, near to the roots. Tie the thread securely in a knot around your hair.

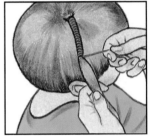

4. Lay one thread along the hair and start to wind the other one neatly around both the hair and the thread.

5. After binding about 5cm (2in), swap the threads over, so that you now bind with the one which was lying along your hair.

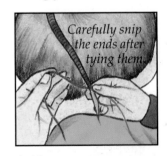

Carefully snip the ends after tying them.

You can tie a hippie braid into your hair even if it's pretty short. See pages 18-19 for other short hair braids.

6. Keep on swapping the threads all the way down. Secure the ends by tying the threads in a small, tight, neat knot.

Joined braids

1. Following the steps for the single hippie braid (see left), make a braid on either side at the front of your head.

2. For a striped effect, bind your hair holding both threads together. Make sure that the threads lie side by side on the braid.

3. Carefully snip the ends of the thread from one of the braids, but leave the two threads attached on the other one.

4. Brush the loose hair, then lay the braids over the top, bringing them together at the back of your head.

5. Join the braids by winding the loose thread around the ends of both braids. Tie the thread with a tight, neat knot.

If your hair is very long you could knot the ends of the braids together rather than securing them with thread.

Tip

You can leave hippie braids in for as long as you like as you can wash them with your hair. When you want to take them out, carefully snip the knot, then gently unravel the threads.

Topknot and knotted bunches

By starting off with simple, familiar styles, such as a ponytail or bunches, you can use the braiding technique to create different hairstyles.

You will need: for the topknot - two covered bands, hairpins, and for the knotted bunches - two covered bands.

Topknot

1. Brush the hair and smooth it into a ponytail on top of your head. Secure it with a covered band.

2. Divide the hair into three equal sections. Braid tightly, until you reach the end of the length of hair.

3. Secure the end of the braid with a covered band. You could wear your hair as a braided ponytail like this.

4. To make the topknot, coil the braid around and around the covered bands until you reach the end.

5. Tuck the end of the braid under the coiled hair. Push the loose ends into the middle of the topknot.

Try to keep your braid as even and neat as you can, as this will make a tidier topknot.

6. To hold the topknot in place, push in several hairpins around the bottom of the braid (see tip box).

Knotted bunches

1. Make a middle part. Push one side out of the way, then divide the other side into three sections.

2. Loosely braid the hair to the end. Secure it tightly with a covered band. Do the same to the other side.

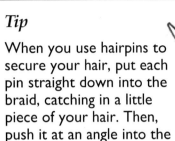

Tip

When you use hairpins to secure your hair, put each pin straight down into the braid, catching in a little piece of your hair. Then, push it at an angle into the middle of the topknot.

To wear your hair in this style you need to braid your hair very loosely, starting level with your ears.

3. Hold the end of one braid and pull it up toward your ear to make a loop. Cross the end over the braid.

4. Pull the end of the braid through the loop to tie a loose knot. Do the same to the other braid.

Cords and ribbons

It's easy to braid cords or ribbons through your hair. You can buy lots of different kinds from department stores. **You will need:** for the cord braid - two covered bands, cord twice as long as your hair; for the ribbon braid - covered band, three ribbons 15cm (6in) longer than your hair, hair clip.

Cord braid

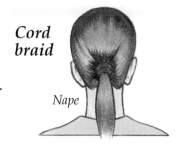

Nape

1. Brush your hair. Gather it into a smooth ponytail at the nape of your neck. Secure it with a covered band.

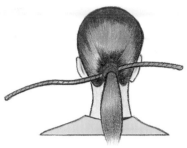

2. Thread the cord through the band under the ponytail. Pull it to make equal lengths on both sides.

Use thin, bright cord which contrasts with your hair.

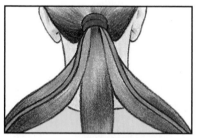

3. Divide the ponytail into three equal sections. Arrange the cord to lie along the two outer pieces of hair.

Secure the cord and the hair with the band.

4. Braid the ponytail, keeping the cord tight with its section of hair. Try to keep the cord on top. Secure with a band.

Tip

If you cut the ends of ribbons on a slant before you use them it stops them from fraying.

When you secure the braid, hide the ends of the cord under the covered band.

Ribbon braid

 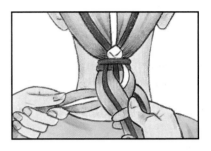

Clip the short ends out of the way.

1. Follow step 1 of the cord braid. Place the ribbons on top of each other and tie a knot 10cm (4in) from one end.

2. Slip the ribbons under a loop in the band with the knot at the top. Divide the hair into three sections, each with a ribbon.

3. Hold each piece of ribbon tightly against its own section of hair as you braid. Try not to twist the ribbon.

Use ribbons which aren't too wide, as they are easier to braid.

4. Secure the hair and ribbons at the end, with a covered band. Tie two of the loose ribbon ends around the band.

5. Unclip the short ends. Cross two of the ribbons under the braid, then tie them neatly over the band.

You could choose ribbons to match the clothes you are wearing.

9

Princess styles

You will need: for the French princess - four fabric bands; for the two-braid princess - two covered bands.

French princess

You can adapt this style by braiding your hair from the blue band to the end.

1. Part off a section of hair across the top of the head. Brush it to make it smooth. Hold it in one hand.

2. Twist a fabric band around this section of hair until it is tight. You could wear your hair like this if you want.

3. Lay the section down on the loose hair. Pick up a new section from behind the ears. Secure it with another band.

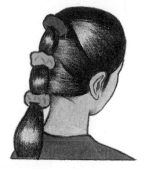

4. Gather all the hair together into a ponytail and secure it with another band at the top of your neck.

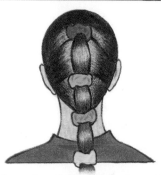

5. Attach a fourth band at the bottom of the hair. Adjust the bands to make them evenly spaced, if you need to.

10

Two-braid princess

1. Use a comb or your fingers to take a section of hair across the crown of your head.

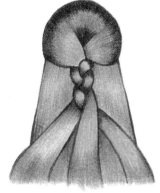

2. Divide the section into three equal parts and braid it to the end. Secure it with a covered band.

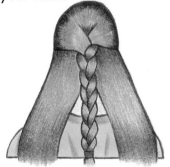

3. Allow the braid to fall straight down. Divide the loose hair into two sections, either side of the braid.

You could also simply wear the braid on top of the loose hair, as it would be at the end of step 3.

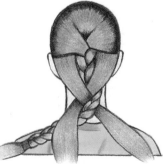

4. Using the braid as one section, braid the hair to the end. Secure tightly with a covered band.

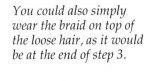

Crossover braids

These two styles are very pretty. You simply need to braid sections of hair and cross them over the top of your head. **You will need:** for the tiara - small covered band, hair clip; for the double crossover - three covered bands. Snap hair clips (see tip) are ideal for securing these braids, because they don't slip out of your hair easily.

Tiara

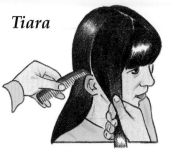

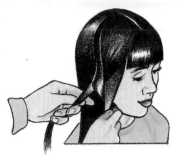

1. Comb the hair and make a middle part. Take a front section of hair and hold it near to the top of your ear.

2. Divide this hair into three equal sections. Braid your hair, keeping the ends pulled down all the time.

Let the hair fall over the ear to hide the hair clip.

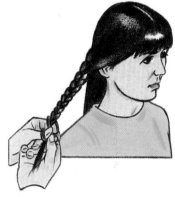

3. Keep your head upright as you braid otherwise the braid won't be even. Secure the end with a covered band.

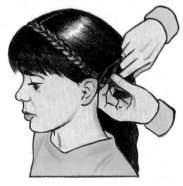

4. Cross the braid over the top of your head, so that the end lies just behind your ear. Secure it with a hair clip.

Double crossover

1. Braid a section at both sides of your head, as for the tiara (see left). Secure the ends with small covered bands.

2. Cross one braid over the top of your head. Take it behind your ear and hold it in place with one hand.

3. Take the other braid over behind the ear on the other side. Make the braids cross neatly on top of the head.

4. Push the loose hair over one shoulder. Bring the ends together at your nape and fasten them with a band.

Tip

If you do a double crossover and your hair isn't long enough to fasten behind your head, use snap hair clips like these to secure the braids behind your ears.

Brush your hair carefully after fastening the braids and let it hang loose.

Six braids

This elaborate style takes quite a long time to braid, but the results are great. Don't leave these tight braids in your hair overnight as it's not very good for your hair and it will be very uncomfortable. **You will need:** one large and six small covered bands, several hairpins.

Use really fine ribbons in the ends of these braids. Tie the ribbons in a double knot, then snip the ends very carefully.

Braids like these are good to wear on a hot day, as all your hair is pulled out of the way.

Tip

If you braid long hair loosely in several sections at bedtime, it helps to prevent tangling. It also makes a lovely ripple of waves through your hair the next day.

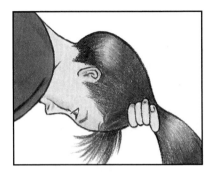

1. Make a high ponytail on top of the head by bending forward and gathering up the hair while it is hanging down.

2. Clasp your hair with your hands and brush it as smooth as you can, before securing it with a covered band.

3. Divide the ponytail into six equal sections. Hold onto one section and push the rest of the hair out of the way.

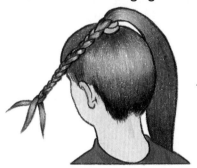

4. Divide this first section of hair into three equal strands. Braid it to the end and secure it with a covered band.

Secure the braid with a band.

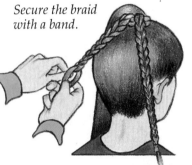

5. Take another section from the loose hair, roughly the same size as the first one. Divide it into three and braid it.

6. Repeat steps 4 and 5 until you have braided all your hair into six braids. Secure each one with a covered band.

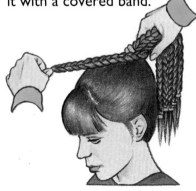

7. Hold five of the braids above your head. Begin to wrap the remaining braid around the covered band.

Wrap it around tightly.

8. Continue wrapping the braid around the base of your braided ponytail until you come to the end.

See page 7 to find out how to use a hairpin.

9. Secure the wound braid by catching small pieces of hair with hairpins and pushing them into the middle of the braids.

Flipover

A flipover at the base of your neck can make an ordinary ponytail look very stylish. You can create this style using a tool called a styler or you can do it with your fingers. **You will need:** for both styles - covered bands.

Flipover using a styler

Add a fabric band to hide the covered one before braiding your ponytail.

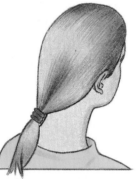

1. Brush the hair well and smooth it into a low ponytail. Secure the ponytail with a covered band.

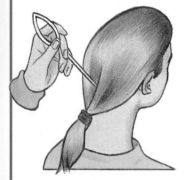

2. Push the point of the styler carefully into the middle of the hair, just above the covered band.

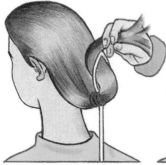

3. Lift up the ponytail and thread it through the loop of the styler. Keep holding onto the end of the ponytail.

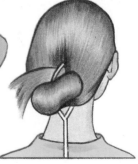

4. Gently pull the styler downward. The ponytail will go through the hair and come out underneath.

5. You can leave the ponytail hanging loose (see right) or you can divide it into three sections and braid it.

Flipover with your hands

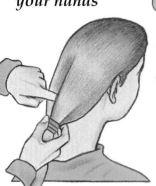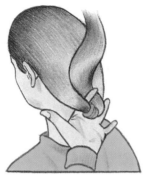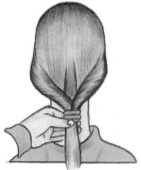

1. Make a low ponytail and secure it. Holding the ponytail, poke a hole through the hair just above the band.

2. Push two fingers from one hand up through the hole and bend the ponytail up with your other hand.

3. Carefully feed the ponytail through the hole with your fingers. Be careful not to let any strands fall free.

4. Pull the ponytail all the way through. Push the band up slightly, then adjust the flipover, so that the band is hidden.

Double flipover

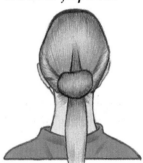

You can do a double flipover, if your hair is long enough, by repeating steps 1 to 4. This creates a bigger rolled effect.

Brush your ponytail really well after flipping it through.

Tip

If you are using a ponystyler, move it from side to side when you push it into the hair (step 2). This makes a gap for the ponytail to flip through.

Shorter hair

Your hair doesn't have to be very long to braid it. There are many styles such as the ones shown here, which you can do on short hair. **You will need:** for the beaded braids - beads with large holes (plastic ones are best as they are lightest), embroidery thread; for the side braid - two small covered bands; for the short French braid - a small covered band.

Here you can see only one braid, but you can do more than one by just repeating the steps below with another strand of hair.

Beaded braids

1. Make a middle part. Pick up a 1cm (½in) section at the part and divide it into three strands.

2. Braid the strands to about 5cm (2in) from the ends. Wet the ends and smooth them together.

3. Thread the bead onto the braid. Grip the end and push the bead up. Add one or two more beads.

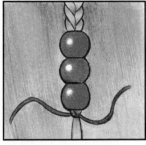

4. Wind 5cm (2in) of thread several times around the end of the braid. Tie the ends of the thread in a knot.

Side braid

1. Take a section of hair from the top of your head. Secure it near to the top with a small covered band.

2. Braid the hair to about 5cm (2in) from the ends of the strands. Secure them tightly with a band.

Thread ribbons through the back of the bands. Tie them in a knot and trim the ends.

Short French braid

1. Make a middle part. Pick up a section of hair between your ear and your forehead. Divide it into three strands and braid it once.

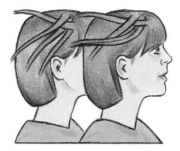

2. Pick up a thin strand from the loose hair below and join it into the right strand. Braid this strand over the strand in the middle.

3. Now pick up a thin strand from the loose hair beside the left strand and join it into the strand. Braid it over the middle one.

4. Repeat steps 2 and 3 once more. Try to keep the braid as tight and neat as you can without pulling your hair too much.

5. Now braid the three strands in the normal way to the end. Secure the braid with a band. Add a ribbon or a scrunchie to hide it.

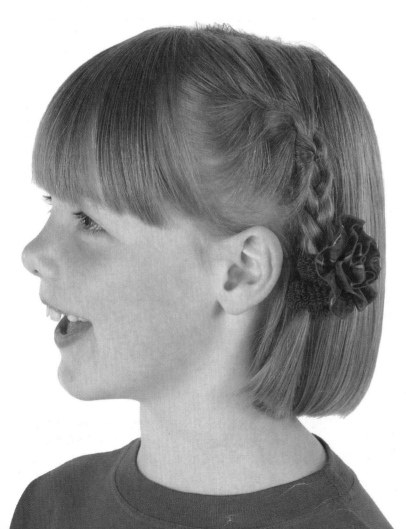

Mini braids

Although this style takes a long time to braid, the results are worth the effort. You can leave the braids in for several days and when you untie them you'll have amazing ripples in your hair. **You will need:** 16 small covered bands, hair clips.

The very fine ribbons at the ends of these braids were slipped through the covered bands, then tied in double bows.

1. Make a middle part, then make another one down to your ear. Make a third part back from the middle of your forehead.

2. Divide the section you have made at the front in two. Braid each section to the end of the hair. Secure them tightly with bands.

3. Lay the two braids you have done over the top of your head. Comb the section of hair beneath these braids. Braid it to the end and secure.

4. Take the part around from above your ear to the back of your head. Divide the hair in two and braid each section, securing them tightly.

Put all the top braids over your head.

This is exactly the same style but with beads added to the ends. You'll need to use beads with large holes in them (see page 18).

5. Make another part level with your ear around to the back part. Divide the section you have made in two and braid each one.

6. Clip the last two braids you tied onto the top of your head. Braid the remaining section of hair which is left between your ear and the back part.

7. Unclip all the braids you have done and let them hang down around your head. Braid all your hair on the other side of your head in the same way.

Tip

Once you have tied your braids, you can wear them in different styles. For high bunches, divide them in two and secure them with thick bands.

21

French braids

There are two ways of creating a French braid. One way is where the braid lies smoothly on the back of the head, and the other "inside-out" technique makes the braid stand out from the head. You'll need to practice a little before you get a really even braid, but it's quick and easy once you have mastered it. **You will need:** for both styles - a covered band.

Try to keep the sections smooth and even as you braid.

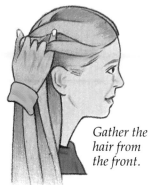

Gather the hair from the front.

1. Pick up and pull back a section of hair from the front of your head. Divide it in three and braid it once.

2. Use one of your fingers to gather up a thin strand from the loose hair next to the right section.

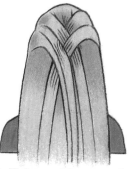

3. Join the strand in neatly with the right section. Cross this over the middle one in the normal way.

4. Take a thin strand from the hair on the left. Join it in with the left strand. Braid it over the middle one.

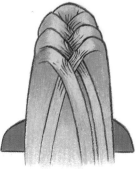

5. Take another thin strand from the loose hair on the right and join it in with the right section. Braid it.

6. Pick up and join in a strand of loose hair with the left section. Braid it over the middle section.

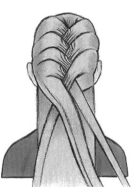

7. Continue braiding tightly in this way, taking a strand of hair from each side to join in with the braid.

The braid forms a ridge down the back of your head.

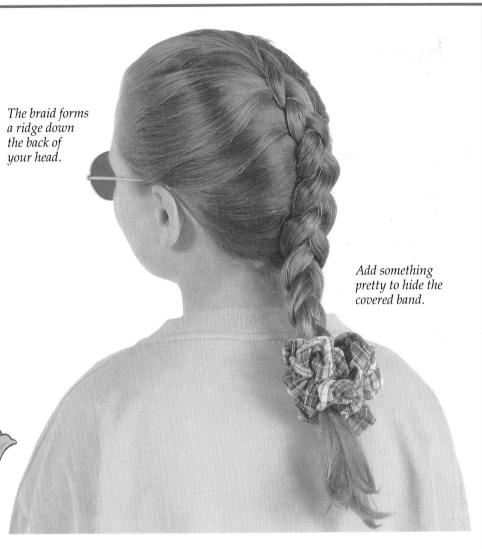

Add something pretty to hide the covered band.

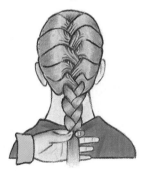

8. At your nape, divide the remaining hair into two sections and join them into the left and right sections.

Inside-out French braid

9. Braid the three strands of hair in the normal way to the end and secure the braid with a covered band.

1. Follow step 1 of the French braid but cross the right and left sections *under*, not over, the middle one.

2. Join in strands of hair in the same way as the French braid, but cross the section *under* the middle one.

Continue to cross the strands under the middle one.

3. At the nape, divide the loose hair and join them in as for the French braid. Braid to the end and secure.

Crown braiding

Crown braids are braided in a similar way to a French braid (see pages 22-23). You can either do one braid across the top of your head, or make several braids running back from your forehead. **You will need:** clip, small covered bands.

Over the top

1. Brush your hair back from your forehead, or from the top of your bangs if you have them.

2. Make a part from ear to ear over your head, so that you make a section about 7cm (3in) wide.

3. Pick up a section from over your left ear. Divide it into three equal strands and braid it once.

4. Pick up a thin strand from the loose hair beneath the right strand. Join it into the right strand.

5. Cross the right strand over the middle one. Pick up a strand and join it in with the left strand. Braid it.

6. Continue to braid over the top of the head, picking up strands and joining them as you go.

7. When you reach the other ear, braid the loose ends of hair in the normal way. Secure with a band.

Straight crown braids

1. Make a section in the middle of the head, about 7cm (3in) deep by 5cm (2in) wide across the head.

2. Divide this hair in two. Clip the back part out of the way, Divide the front piece into three strands.

3. Hold the strands firmly. Take the right strand over the middle and then left over the middle.

4. Unclip the back part. Pick up two thin strands from the back section. Join them to the outer sections.

5. Braid the hair once, then pick up two more strands from the back section and braid the hair again.

6. Continue braiding in this way until you reach the back of the section. Secure the braid with a small band.

The loose hair has been fluffed up behind the braids.

Braid as many sections as you like around your head.

7. Make another section parallel with the first one. Braid this section of hair following steps 2 to 6.

Five-strand braid

This style looks far more complicated than it is to do. You braid with five strands of hair rather than with three. At first, you may find it easier to have two people hold the braid. Your hair needs to be fairly long for this style to be successful. **You will need:** a covered band.

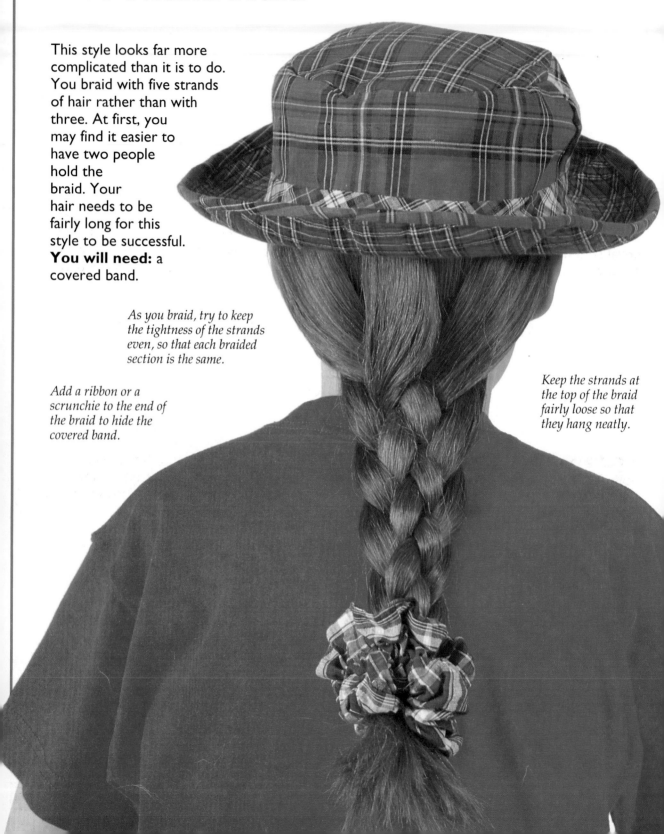

As you braid, try to keep the tightness of the strands even, so that each braided section is the same.

Add a ribbon or a scrunchie to the end of the braid to hide the covered band.

Keep the strands at the top of the braid fairly loose so that they hang neatly.

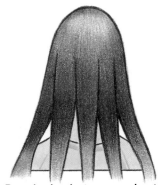

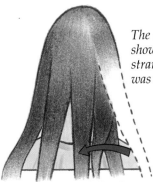

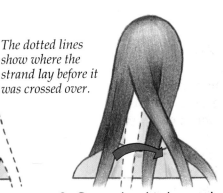

The dotted lines show where the strand lay before it was crossed over.

1. Brush the hair to make it smooth. Divide it into five equal strands. Arrange them around the shoulders.

2. Begin to braid the hair loosely, by crossing the first strand on the right over the second strand.

3. Cross the third strand over the second one. Don't try to hold all the strands, just lay them loosely across the back.

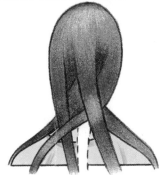

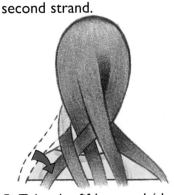

4. Cross the strand which is now in the middle, over the fourth one. Keep the strands fairly loose as you braid.

5. Take the fifth strand (the one on the left) over the fourth one. This completes the braiding pattern.

6. Starting with the first strand again, continue the braiding pattern, following steps 2 to 5.

You'll need to hold the ends of the strands as they get shorter.

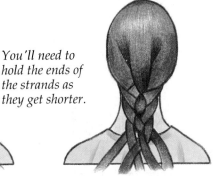

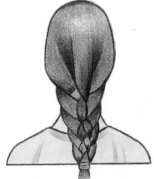

7. Your hair should look like this after completing the braiding pattern for the second time.

8. Keep on following the pattern as many times as you can. Try to keep the strands pulled evenly.

9. When you get to the end of the hair, pull all the strands together and secure them with a covered band.

Rope braid

This braid looks really great and very different from a normal three-strand braid. It is easiest to do if you have two people to hold your hair. If you are left-handed, reverse all the instructions so that you twist the hair toward the right and cross the right section over both twists each time. **You will need:** two covered bands.

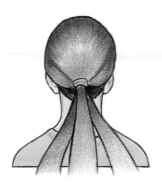

1. Brush the hair back smoothly into a ponytail and secure it with a covered band. Divide the ponytail into three equal sections.

2. Take the right strand and twist it tightly around toward the left. Continue this until you have twisted the whole length.

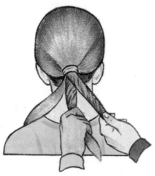

3. Ask someone to hold the right strand, keeping it twisted and held out straight. Twist the middle strand around to the left too.

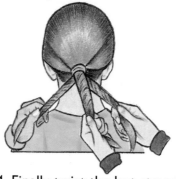

4. Finally twist the last strand around to the left, so that all three strands are twisted. Get your assistant to hold the right and middle ones.

5. Take the left strand and cross it all the way over the other two strands. Hold the strands tightly otherwise the twists will begin to unravel.

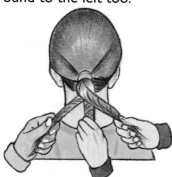

6. Carefully swap your hands around so that your assistant is holding the middle strand and the one which is now on the right, as in step 4.

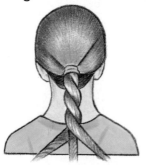

7. Continue down the hair in this way, always crossing the strand on the left over the other two and swapping your hands around each time.

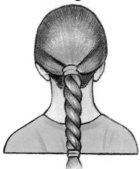

8. At the end of the braid, join the strands together, holding them tightly. Secure with a covered band.

Add a scrunchie or a ribbon to hide the covered band at the bottom of the braid.

Tying a neat bow

Tie a knot.

1. Slip the ribbon through a loop of your covered band, under the braid.

Loose end

2. Make the ribbons into loops, leaving an extra loose piece at the end.

3. Cross the loops over, with the left loop on top of the right one.

4. Bring the left loop up between the right loop and the knot. Pull the loops.

Fishtail braids

Fishtail braids are a different kind of braid, using just two sections. They look very intricate but they aren't as difficult to do as they might seem, although they are not that easy to do on yourself. **You will need:** for one fishtail braid - covered band; for the bunches - two covered bands.

Fishtail

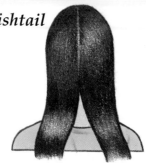

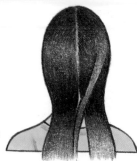

1. Brush the hair smoothly. Divide the hair into two equal sections down the back of the head.

2. Hold the hair in your left hand as shown. Pick up a thin strand from the outside of the right section.

3. Cross the strand over and join it into the inside of the left section of hair. Smooth it together.

Add a ribbon or a scrunchie to cover the band at the end of your fishtail.

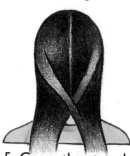

4. Swap the sections to your right hand and take a fine strand from the outside of the left section.

5. Cross the strand over to join the inside of the right section. Smooth it in with the hair of this section.

6. Repeat steps 2 to 5, working down the braid. Keep the thickness of the fine strands even.

7. When you reach the bottom of the hair, secure the end of the braid tightly in a covered band.

Fishtail bunches

I. Make a middle part. Push one side out of the way. Divide the other side into two sections.

2. Take a thin strand from the outside of the left section. Cross it over to join the right section.

3. Pick up a fine strand from the outside of the right section. Take it over to join into the inside of the left one.

4. Continue braiding crossing a right, then a left strand over and joining it in. Secure the end with a band.

5. Divide the other side into two equal sections. Braid it in the same way starting with a right section.

Start the bunches off very loosely then keep the strands neat and tight.

Tip

When you do a fishtail braid, make sure that you keep the hair pulled firmly downward and not out at an angle. This will help you to keep all the strands in a neat and even pattern.

Braid your fishtail bunches behind your ear.

Accessories

This page shows you a selection of the accessories you need to secure your braids. There are also some accessories which you can add to your braids to make them bright and fun. Most department stores sell a large variety of different kinds, but you can often buy them cheaply from discount stores.

Covered bands come in all kinds of sizes and thicknesses. Use a small one on a fine braid and a larger one to secure a chunky braid.

Snap hair clips can be used to clip loose hair out of the way and for securing crossover braids.

Choose bright embroidery threads for hippie braids.

Very thin ribbons look great in the ends of fine braids.

Small fabric band

Use thick ribbons to tie a big neat bow at the end of a thick braid.

Thin cord

Fabric bands

Hair pins

Beads for adding to the ends of thin braids.

You can buy scrunchies made from all kinds of attractive fabrics.